APPRENTICESHIP END POINT ASSESSMENT SUCCESS

Customer Service Practitioner EPA

Apprenticeship Course Code ST0072

Louise Webber

DEDICATION

This book is dedicated to the apprenticeship students and employers I have worked with over the years, for their hard work, support and determination.

CONTENTS

1 INTRODUCTION AND HOW TO USE THIS BOOK

Congratulations! If you are reading this book then you have very likely landed your apprenticeship job, completed your on-programme study and now you have reached the point where you need to pass your end-point assessment (EPA) so that you can claim that all-important apprenticeship completion certificate.

After getting your apprenticeship job, passing your end-point assessment (known as EPA) is probably the most important part of your apprenticeship.

This book is designed to support you with the required preparation for your EPA and give you a great understanding of the EPA requirements and what you need to do to succeed.

The most important sections for you to study in detail are sections 8, 9 and 10. These sections go into detail about each element of your EPA. For the Customer Service Practitioner EPA there are three requirements:

- Apprentice Showcase, section 8
- Practical Observation, section 9
- Professional Discussion, section 10

To make the most of this book, it should be read in its entirety, but these three sections will detail the specific information you need to pass, or achieve distinction, in each of the areas. You will need to pass each individual area to pass your EPA.

Each of these sections should be reviewed and checked prior to your EPA and prior to submission of your showcase document.

The EPA is an opportunity for you to show all the skills and knowledge you have acquired over your time on the course. This book will support you in feeling prepared, organised and confident in your EPA. You will then have all the information you need to pass your EPA and to complete your apprenticeship.

Throughout the book, you will learn about EPA, the strategies you can use to be successful, required preparation and how to cope with the stress and pressure that EPA can put on students.

This book will explain what the EPA assessor will be looking for and how each area is graded. This will enable you to be as prepared as you possibly can be for your EPA to get the best possible result.

This book will focus not only on how to pass your EPA, but the preparation, skills and knowledge required for you to achieve a distinction.

It is important that you see your EPA as an opportunity to shine. It is a chance to show off your skills and knowledge. If you see EPA in this way, then it takes the mental pressure off somewhat and can give you a positive attitude towards the assessment. Have a think about when you have done exams in the past. Often, those around you who were confident and relaxed, but organised and prepared, were those who obtained the best results. Getting stressed and nervous can have a very detrimental effect on examination outcomes.

This book will assist you in full preparation for your EPA, as well as giving you support in calming your nerves, timing your EPA for the best possible outcome and providing you with practice material.

EPA is an important development within apprenticeships. Passing your EPA shows that you have completed your on-programme work and assessment and also that you have shown an independent, completely detached assessor that you are worthy of passing your apprenticeship.

Whilst apprenticeships have been around for years, EPA is new, not only to you, but to your apprenticeship provider, the EPA assessment organisations and your personal tutor. So, the more you know about it in advance, the better prepared you are likely to be and the more chance of you passing your EPA with the grade you are looking for.

Having a good understanding of what your EPA assessor is looking for, the requirements for the standard and how best to present your work will give you a great start to your EPA.

Passing your EPA is essential and you cannot complete your Customer Service Practitioner apprenticeship without passing your EPA.

This book will not teach you to be a good Customer Service Practitioner. It is not designed to. The purpose of this book is to support you in preparing for your EPA and in getting the best possible result you can. Your training provider, employer and tutor should already have taught you all you need to know about customer service before you reach EPA stage.

Prior to your EPA, you should have been well supported through the 20% off the job training time, as well as gaining valuable practical work experience.

EPA is one of the biggest changes that followed recent apprenticeship reform. Previously, apprentices worked towards 'apprenticeship frameworks' and would be continually assessed throughout their apprenticeship (like coursework only qualifications, such as some Btec courses). All work would be marked by the assessor/tutor who worked with, coached and trained the apprentice. This work was then checked by a senior member of the team, called an internal verifier. The internal verifier (who normally works for the same organisation as your personal tutor) had the authority to approve the apprentice's work for completion and certification.

Some of the work produced by apprentices at the training centre or college would have been checked by examination boards through sampling of portfolios. Of course Ofsted, Ofqual and funding providers can also inspect the quality of work produced by apprentices and the support functions offered by training centres and colleges.

The employer groups, who designed the new apprenticeship standards, wanted to make apprenticeships more robust and for the final sign off to be more independent and therefore introduced this additional checking system, which is the EPA. The apprentice's work (or at least some of it) is now assessed by an external assessor, with a view to making the results more credible, independent, reliable and more suitable to the needs of the customer service industry.

Following the implementation of the new apprenticeship standards (like the Customer Service Practitioner Apprenticeship Standard), the old apprenticeship frameworks are now being slowly phased out and replaced by these new courses, which, of course, require EPA by an external organisation. The aim of this is to reduce any actual, or perceived, conflict of interest in apprenticeship successes and pass rates.

This is a massive change for apprenticeship providers, as not only course requirements have been updated, but there is now a whole new system of completion for apprenticeships, which is the 'gateway' and then the EPA.

This is good news for you, as an apprentice. Your apprenticeship course is not only nationally recognised, and recently updated, but also demonstrates that you will have proven your skills, ability and knowledge to a complete stranger, who has no vested interest in your success or otherwise. This adds even more credibility to your achievement as a Customer Service Practitioner and therefore adds more weight to your CV, which in turn should improve your long-term career prospects.

During your apprenticeship, as a Customer Service Practitioner, you will still complete a portfolio of evidence. Continual assessment of this will still take place in a similar way to the old apprenticeship frameworks. However, with the new standards, apprentices will now take an EPA in order to complete the apprenticeship.

Apprentices cannot be signed off their Customer Service Practitioner apprenticeship by the training provider or college with whom they have studied their on-programme element of the course. The EPA assessor, and the end point assessment company they work for, must be completely independent, not known to you personally or worked with you as a tutor.

The EPA is designed to test whether the apprentice has gained the skills, knowledge and behaviours outlined in the apprenticeship standard. Once you pass your EPA then you have passed your apprenticeship.

Most apprenticeships, including the old Customer Service Level 2 Apprenticeship Framework, were not graded, and apprentices either passed or did not pass.

The Customer Service Practitioner Level 2 Standard Apprenticeship, gives apprentices the opportunity to achieve a pass, fail or distinction grade. This is a fantastic development, as previously there were substantial differences in the quality of work produced by customer service apprentices, which was not fully recognised. As an internal verifier myself, I have seen massive differences in the quality of work produced by apprentices. Whilst it is often the case that apprentices were asked to complete additional work to get to the standard needed, there was no real recognition for high achievers, which seemed a little unfair to those who produced excellent or outstanding work. This has been rectified with the introduction of the EPA.

The apprenticeship reforms looked to update apprenticeship requirements as well as the system of grading. The standards have been put together by employer groups, so the idea is that they are more robust, more modern and more relevant to the needs of industry. Customer service, like many other industries has changed substantially over recent years, with improvements in technology and on-line services, as well as with the changing demands of customers in modern society.

The new standard qualification reflects these changes. It has flexibility for learners in every sector of customer service, and for whatever types of customer the apprentices may be dealing with.

The reforms were not only important for updating the qualification in line with changes in the industry, but also the government were looking for an additional layer of verification within the process to maintain the integrity of apprenticeships. The EPA organisation provides this additional level of checking and verification of apprentice's work.

The EPA assessor will check that the apprentice meets all the requirements of the apprenticeship as part of the 'gateway' to EPA. He or she will then assess the learner to ensure they have the skills, knowledge and competences required to meet the standard.

Normally as an apprentice, you will be supported by your personal tutor and your employer, with whom you have (hopefully) developed a strong working relationship and feel very comfortable with. Your EPA assessor will be a complete stranger, and they will be observing you at work, marking your showcase portfolio and conducting a professional discussion with you, to verify that you are competent to be 'signed off' as a Customer Service

Practitioner.

This is a big deal for many apprentices. A complete stranger checking your work and watching you! This is not most people's idea of fun, but by following the hints, tips and guidance in this book, and with the support and guidance of your personal tutor and employer, you will put yourself in the best possible position you can to pass your EPA without any issues.

Your EPA assessor will not work for your college or training provider and will not be known to you personally. The EPA assessor has to be completely impartial. EPA assessment centres are duty bound to ensure that their assessors do not have a vested interest in the learner passing their EPA. The EPA centre will have a 'conflict of interest' policy in place, meaning that they need to check before allocating you an EPA assessor, that he or she has not worked with you in the past and does not know you personally.

All EPA organisations must pass an application process with the ESFA (Education and Skills Funding Agency) in order to be able to deliver EPA assessments. Part of this process makes sure that the centre has strict procedures in place to prevent conflict of interest and that the centre (and the staff who work for them) have a good understanding of the customer service industry.

EPA organisations will be listed on the 'Register of End Point Assessment Organisations'. Your employer with the support of the training provider or college you work with will chose which EPA organisation to use for your EPA.

Currently there are not that many to choose from! As of September 2018, there are 166 EPA organisations on the register and only 15 approved for the Customer Service Practitioner Apprenticeship Standard. Centres also need to be approved by Ofqual in order to deliver EPA for this apprenticeship, which is a very lengthy process, which may be part of the reason why there are so few centres offering this service.

The EPA assessor and assessment organisation will be experienced in the delivery of customer service. All EPA assessors are required to complete CPD (continuous professional development), which means that they keep their knowledge and understanding of the customer service industry up to date.

Your role, as a customer service practitioner, is to deliver high quality products or services to the customers at your place of work.

Customer service can be delivered digitally, face-to-face or by telephone. Customer service tasks may be one-off or routine and normally include dealing with orders, payments, queries, complaints, after service, resolving customer issues or gaining an insight into customer needs through measuring customer satisfaction.

Your role may mean that often you are the customers' first point of contact and your actions can, and will, influence the customer experience and levels of satisfaction with the company you work for as an apprentice.

You will need to demonstrate excellent customer service skills, good product knowledge and the ability to work within company rules and guidelines, when dealing with customers.

Your EPA assessor will be very experienced in all these areas and will be looking for you to show the skills and knowledge you have gained whilst on your course.

2 THE TOP 10 REASONS TO MAKE SURE YOU PASS YOUR END POINT ASSESSMENT

You need to complete your end-point assessment so that you can show that you have fully completed and passed your apprenticeship.

Let's look at the top 10 reasons to pass your EPA:

1. You cannot complete your Customer Service Practitioner apprenticeship without passing the EPA.

2. The more qualifications you have on your CV the stronger it will be and the better your career prospects.

3. A sense of achievement and accomplishment.

4. Once you have passed your EPA you may be offered a progression course by your training provider which will give you even more skills, knowledge and experience to add to your CV.

5. Your employer will have invested time, money, support and guidance during your

apprenticeship and they will want you to succeed. As your employer pays your wages it is a good idea to reward his/her support with your achievement.

6. When you complete your EPA you will receive a certificate from the ESFA. Many EPA centres also offer EPA completion certificates too.

7. Your training provider has been a source of support for you over the last 12 months. They want you to succeed and will support you through the process.

8. The EPA is a chance to show off all the good work you have done over the time you have been on your apprenticeship.

9. The assessment process is good experience for you. Overcoming any nerves and preparing your work for EPA will help you to prepare for similar events in the future.

10. You now have the opportunity to pass your apprenticeship, or even achieve a distinction, which looks great when you are looking for work in the future.

In addition, you may qualify for a pay increase once you have fully completed your apprenticeship!

3 GETTING PREPARED FOR THE GATEWAY

The 'Gateway' is when you, as an apprentice, show that you are ready for your EPA and that you are ready to fully complete your apprenticeship.

The image below, which is shown in the assessment plan for the Customer Service Practitioner Apprenticeship Standard, shows the structure of the programme and where the gateway comes in.

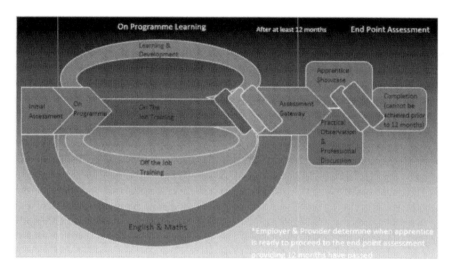

To go through the gateway, you must have completed all of the following areas:

- Completed all of the 'on-programme' element of the apprenticeship, including any Btec or NVQ qualifications that have been built into your course, if applicable.

- Passed maths and English functional skills at level 1. In addition, you must have at least attempted to pass at level 2 (or have equivalent GCSEs or similar). Your training provider will need to send evidence of this to the end-point assessment organisation.

- Have photographic identification to show the end-point assessment organisation who you are. You will need a driving license or passport if you have them. Your training provider will supply you with a list of other identification that can be used if you don't have either of these.

- Proof that you, your employer and training provider, agree that you are ready for your EPA and that you have met all the gateway entry requirements. You will very likely have a form to complete to send to your end point assessment organisation. This form will have to be signed by all parties.

- You must have been on your apprenticeship programme for at least 12 months prior to the gateway.

4 END POINT ASSESSMENT ORGANISATIONS

An independent organisation must be involved in the end-point assessment of each apprentice. This is so that all apprentices following the same standard are assessed consistently and fairly.

The independence of the EPA organisation also ensures that there is no conflict of interest. This means that apprentices who pass their EPA have done so on their own merit and according to high standards. This helps to ensure that the apprenticeship qualification is worthy and will continue to be a nationally recognised and well-respected qualification.

It is important for you to know that you are gaining a qualification which is held in high regard. Don't be afraid of the EPA. It is an important verification process to make sure that only those apprentices who deserve the qualification will be awarded it.

Only organisations on the register of end-point assessment organisations are authorised to conduct independent end-point assessment of apprentices.

The number of end-point assessment organisations is growing all the time. Your employer, with support from your training provider or college, will select an end-point assessment organisation from the list of approved centres.

In September 2018 there were only 15 end-point assessment organisations to choose from for your Customer Service Practitioner apprenticeship. Currently, the end-point assessment organisations do not have much competition. However, as EPA is now a requirement of all apprenticeship standards then more companies will apply to be on the register.

All end-point assessment organisations have been through a rigorous application process to be able to deliver EPAs. As EPA is so new, it is almost impossible to compare centres and there is no success rate data available yet to help you decide which EPA centre to use.

There are some considerations which you may want to think about regarding which EPA centre to use. It is the employer's decision but if you have any say in which EPA company your employer/training provider use you could consider the following:

Local companies: Might be more familiar with local dialect, accents etc. & it may be easier to arrange re-sits if required.

The type of company: You might prefer to work with an EPA company that are also a training provider, as they might understand more what an apprentice goes through. Alternatively, you might prefer an EPA centre who are also an examination board.

EPA centres must be impartial, so if you know an EPA assessor, you must disclose this and have another assessor allocated to you or use an alternative centre.

You may or may not be able to influence which EPA centre you use. Just be mindful that you cannot use one with whom you have trained before. You cannot be assessed by an EPA assessor with whom you have any personal relationship with or who has trained you.

All the centres will be delivering the same sort of assessments and so the choice may be largely dependent on costings for the employer/training provider.

You can find details of end-point assessment centres on the websites below:

https://www.gov.uk/guidance/register-of-end-point-assessment-organisations

https://findapprenticeshiptraining.sfa.bis.gov.uk/Apprenticeship/Standard/122?keywords=adult%20care

5 TRAINING PROVIDER SUPPORT AND GUIDANCE

Your training provider should be able to provide you with support and guidance to help you prepare for your EPA. Your personal tutor should supply you with support material and resources to help you prepare for the three elements of your EPA.

In terms of your practical observation, your training provider can support you by conducting a mock observation. Some centres offer mock observations to be carried out by a different assessor, so, someone other than the normal assessor/tutor you have trained with. This will give you experience of how it feels to be observed by a stranger. This can be a very effective method of ensuring that apprentices feel at ease when it comes to the final EPA observation and may help you to overcome test day nerves.

Your centre should also provide you with checklists of exactly what you need to do when you are being observed. This information is also available in this book in the section which goes into detail about the practical observation element of the EPA (section 9).

Your personal tutor will also support you in putting together your apprentice showcase. You have different options regarding how you can deliver the showcase and we shall go into more detail about this in section 8 later in this book.

Use you tutor as much as you can to make sure your showcase is as good as it possibly can be. This will most likely be the first thing the EPA sees from you and people naturally make first impressions so you want them to be good ones.

Your tutor will be (or should be) a customer service expert. They also know what is needed and will help you prepare, so make the most of their knowledge, support and experience.

Make sure you have plenty of time to spend with your tutor in the run up to your EPA. Often apprentices make less time for the tutor towards the end of their apprenticeship as they feel they need them less as they are becoming more proficient at their job role and at completing self-study assignments.

EPA preparation is a time that you really do need your tutor – you don't want to have to re-sit your EPA. If you do have to re-sit, your grade might be capped at a pass mark, rather than giving you the opportunity to gain a distinction. Be certain to show your tutor your showcase in plenty of time. Make the most of support visits and workshop training sessions.

As with the observation, the professional discussion can be rehearsed as well.

It is a good idea to use professional discussion as part of your on-programme work and it also saves time writing assignments if you have voice recorded them. This gets you used to answering questions verbally and will also help you to get a good idea of how much detail to go into for a level 2 professional discussion answer.

If your tutor has not suggested a professional discussion as part of your on-programme work, it might be a good idea for you to suggest it. Many apprentices' portfolios are now on e-portfolio with apps to support with the gathering of evidence. If you have an e-portfolio, you might even be able to voice record answers to your knowledge and understanding questions and upload for your tutor to check. Have a chat with your tutor and see if they can support you with this.

Even if you don't use professional discussion as part of your on programme evidence, it's a good idea to try this out in advance of your EPA. Your tutor may be able to arrange for another assessor/tutor to conduct a mock professional discussion so that you get used to answering questions to complete strangers.

You can then get feedback as to whether they think you would have passed your EPA for this section and if not, you can then repeat the mock assessments until you and your tutor feel you are at a standard where you should now pass or achieve a distinction.

Ask your tutor if they have any resources to help you prepare. They may have model answers or even showcase examples. Of course, yours needs to be personal to you anyway so you can't copy but it might give you the confidence to know that you are headed in the right direction.

6 BOOKING YOUR END POINT ASSESSMENT

Planning for your EPA is important so that you have some control of when, where and how your EPA is conducted.

You can ask your training provider to book your EPA well in advance of when you need it. That way you have secured your date and the EPA organisation you, your employer or training provider have a preference for.

As the current numbers of EPA organisations is very low, recommendations would be to book up early or you may find that you are left waiting to complete your apprenticeship if you cannot secure an assessment date.

If you are kept waiting this can affect a potential pay increase as your employer may not want to increase your salary until you have been fully signed off as an apprentice. In addition, you might miss out on development opportunities that come by as you are not ready to progress as quickly as you would like. Not only that, if you leave it too long you might have forgotten some of the learning that you have done and have to spend extra revision and refresher time to prepare.

If all is going well on your apprenticeship and you are either on, or ahead of your progression target, then you could look to book your EPA date when you are around nine months into your apprenticeship.

You are not permitted to take your EPA until you have been on programme for at least twelve months but it is always good to get a date in the diary.

Your employer or training provider will have to pay for your EPA. This is a substantial amount of money so it is important that you pass first time if possible. Therefore, you need to be as well prepared as you can be and follow the guidance suggestions in this book and the information given to you by your training provider, personal tutor and EPA centre/assessor.

Another reason to book your EPA well in advance is so that you have more choice of what day and time the EPA will take place. This is particularly important with the observation part of the EPA, which will be discussed in more detail in section 9 of this book.

You will need to pick a time and location for your EPA observation which will show you at your best. Have a think about when you are most busy at work. Does this show you giving the best possible customer service? Would a quieter time work better for you? There may be times when you have no customers at all to serve at work so this would be a terrible time to book your EPA observation as the observer would have literally nothing to observe and so cannot possibly pass you.

Have a think about which EPA organisation you think would suit you best. Whilst they all must comply with strict guidelines on how to deliver the EPA, you might feel more comfortable with one type of organisation than another. You might feel more comfortable with an assessor who is from your local area for example, who might be more in tune with local accents or colloquialisms. You might prefer to use an end-point assessment organisation who is also a training provider or an employer.

EPA organisations that already train apprentices will have a good understanding of the requirements of the standard and what apprentices go through. Obviously, your own training provider can't be your EPA organisation, as they could be seen to be biased in your favour so you have to use an EPA organisation you haven't worked with during your training.

You will need to talk to your training provider and employer as they are the people with the authority to book your EPA for you.

In summary:

- Speak to your tutor about booking your EPA when you have around 3 months left on programme (if you are on target and have completed functional skills).

- Try to choose a date and time for your observation when you are likely to have sufficient customers to serve and not too many that you might become flustered.

- Talk to your tutor, employer or training provider about which EPA organisation they are planning to use and why they have selected them.

7 OVERVIEW OF THE EPA FOR THE CUSTOMER SERVICE PRACTITIONER APPRENTICESHIP

The aim of the End Point Assessment (EPA) is to ensure that the apprentice has achieved the required levels of knowledge, skills and competence in their role as a customer service practitioner. The end-point assessment is to verify that the standards set have been met in all areas.

A customer service practitioner is required to be able to deliver high quality service and/or products to customers within their organisation. This could include taking customer orders, taking payments, meeting and greeting customers, offering advice and/or support, sales, complaint handling, aftersales or other suitable customer service-based tasks.

Customer service can be delivered face to face, online or at a customer's own premises. It can also include social media.

Customer service practitioners should be able to provide a high level of customer service in line with their organisations standards, procedures and working methods as well as in line with any appropriate regulatory requirements. As a customer service practitioner, first impressions matter and customer service practitioners should be aware that their actions can influence the customers' experience and impression of the organisation they are representing.

In order to fully achieve this apprenticeship, learners are required to:

- Complete their on-programme period of learning and development
- Pass their End Point Assessment
- Obtain a Pass/Distinction as part of the End Point Assessment

The End Point Assessment is made up of three components:

1. Apprentice showcase

2. Practical observation

3. Professional discussion

For each of the three assessment methods, all pass criteria (100%) must be achieved to progress and to complete the apprenticeship programme.

To be awarded a distinction, you must pass all of the pass criteria, plus a percentage of the distinction criteria in each assessment method as outlined in the table below:

Assessment Method	Weighting	Duration	To achieve a pass	To achieve a Distinction
Apprentice Showcase	65%	After a minimum of 12 months on-programme learning	100%	You must meet all of the pass criteria AND 70% of the distinction criteria
Practical Observation	20%	Minimum of 1 hour	100%	You must meet all of the pass criteria AND 80% of the distinction criteria
Professional Discussion	15%	1 hour	100%	You must meet all of the pass criteria AND 75% of the

Normally the apprentice showcase will be sent to the EPA assessment centre first. This is because this can be marked and checked before going through the other areas of the EPA.

It is normal practice for the practical observation to be completed next and then the professional discussion will be the final area to be covered.

The professional discussion is normally left until last so that any areas that were weak, or not seen, in the other elements of the EPA can be discussed and covered off via the discussion.

The professional discussion gives the EPA assessor a final opportunity to find any outstanding evidence to support the apprentice in passing or in reaching a distinction grade.

The EPA for this standard contains 18 sections. To make this easier to break down each section has been labelled according to the letters of the alphabet. The section numbers are for the purpose of this book (and not on the assessment plan) and are there purely to help you to plan for your EPA.

The actual assessment plan does not give alphabetical references to the standards but doing so can help you to organise your work more efficiently and effectively.

Section	Standard	Element of the EPA this will be assessed by
A	Knowing your customers	Professional discussion
B	Understanding the organisation	Apprentice showcase
C	Meeting regulations and legislation	Apprentice showcase
D	Systems and resources	Apprentice showcase
E	Your role and responsibility	Professional discussion
F	Customer experience	Professional discussion

G	Product and service knowledge	Apprentice showcase
H	Interpersonal skills	Observation
I	Communication	Observation
J	influencing skills	Apprentice showcase
K	Personal organisation	Apprentice showcase
L	Dealing with customer conflict and challenge	Apprentice showcase
M	Developing self	Apprentice showcase
N	Being open to feedback	Apprentice showcase
O	Team working	Apprentice showcase
P	Equality – treating all customers as individuals	Observation
Q	Presentation – dress code, professional language	Observation
R	Right first time	Observation

8 EPA APPRENTICE SHOWCASE

The apprentice showcase is literally a chance for you to showcase, or show off, all the skills and knowledge you have learned during your Customer Service Practitioner apprenticeship.

The apprentice showcase is weighted at a massive 65% of your entire EPA. So, you need to make sure it's good. To achieve a pass, you need to meet 100% of the criteria.

To achieve a distinction, you need to meet all of the pass criteria and 70% of the distinction criteria as well.

Showcase grade summary:

Pass = 100%, Distinction = ALL of the pass marks and 7 out of 10 of the distinction criteria

---

You should begin work on your showcase at the end of your apprenticeship, so in effect, after the 12 months is up.

However, there is nothing stopping you from starting to collate information and evidence in preparation for creating your showcase and this will help to save you time later.

Below is an extract taken from the assessment plan document for the Customer Service Practitioner Standard:

'*The apprentice showcase will be assessed against an externally set brief, written by the assessment organisation, working with employers and other stakeholders, as appropriate, to ensure consistency.*

It is expected that the externally set brief will include elements such as work-based evidence, including customer feedback, recordings, manager statements and witness statements. It will also include evidence from others, such as mid and end of year performance reviews and feedback. It is important to acknowledge that the employer and training provider will work together throughout the on-programme learning, ensuring all learning is consistently applied throughout the apprenticeship and not just at the end point assessment or in the apprentice showcase.

The apprentice will then present to the independent assessor to provide an opportunity for them to interview the apprentice and delve deeper in to the learning and experience. This is to ensure rigor, competence and independence.'

This means the end point assessment organisation that you are working with for your EPA will set specific guidelines on how the showcase is to be delivered. However, all will have similarities in what they ask you to do for your showcase. Make sure to ask your tutor to get as much information as they can from your end point assessment organisation so that you have an exact idea of their requirements.

Gather the following evidence in preparation for collating your showcase. One or two pieces of evidence for each area will give you a good start:

- Feedback from your tutor/assessor
- Witness statements
- Your performance appraisal and performance reviews
- Manager statements
- Recordings of your dealings with customers
- Customer feedback

Note: Whilst your tutor may have observed you at work delivering customer service and written up an observation report, it is recommended that you do not submit this as evidence for your showcase as some EPA centres may not accept this evidence.

You will provide evidence of your skills, knowledge and competency in customer service. You will also need to demonstrate how you have applied your learning and training into work-based tasks. This means that you need to relate what you put in your showcase to your own place of work and job role. I cannot stress enough how important this is. It is your showcase, not 'stuff off the internet' and you need to make it personal.

Remember, as with all three EPA assessment methods, there is an opportunity for pass or distinction grades (and fail, but let's face it, we are seriously looking to avoid even going there).

As an apprentice, you will need to:

- Demonstrate your knowledge and understanding of the principles and practices laid out in the standard and how these are applied in your work role
- Provide evidence to demonstrate your competence in using systems, equipment and technology to deliver customer service (work-based product evidence)
- Identify customers' needs and how they have met those needs and provide evidence of how you have achieved this
- Provide evidence of dealing with challenging customers and conflict
- Provide evidence to show you are working effectively with others
- Provide evidence to show how you manage and are managing your own personal development

This evidence will need to be submitted via a showcase portfolio. The evidence contained in the showcase will be assessed by the EPA assessor against the following areas:

- Understanding the organisation
- Meeting regulations and legislation
- Systems and resources
- Product and service knowledge
- Influencing skills
- Personal organisation
- Dealing with customer conflict and challenge
- Developing self
- Being open to feedback
- Team working

Your showcase portfolio should be in a format in which it can be sent electronically, such as a word document, PowerPoint or PDF.

Alternatively, many EPA organisations will allow apprentices to produce a presentation, which could be video recorded and submitted along with copies of the presentation slides and notes as required.

It should take you around 10-12 hours to complete your showcase of evidence. It may take less time or longer to complete depending on how fast you work, any research required and how much you 'know your stuff'.

If you think it through, you will be likely to need at least 2 solid days to prepare your showcase, maybe more. Alternatively, you could work on it for 4 half days or for an hour each day for several days.

How you manage your time is up to you and your employer. Personally, I would start working on the knowledge questions first, get these out of the way and then begin collating the evidence of my behaviour and work performance, but how you work on it is a matter of personal preference. Just be prepared that you will have to put in fair amount of effort to get the result you are looking for.

You may use the internet for research in preparation for your showcase but your work must be your own and evidence of plagiarism will mean that work submitted will not be accepted. Assessors now have some very clever tools to check for evidence of plagiarism!

It is good to look up theory and they work of others but always make sure that your work is original and personalised to you. This means that your work will always be authentic and you can never be accused of copying. I know I have laboured this point, but it really is a big one, so please take note.

A really quick way of researching information is by using Google Images. Sometimes Google Images will give you an idea of where to start if you don't understand something. That doesn't mean you should put them into your showcase but if you are struggling with an answer it can often provide a good visual clue.

If you opt to deliver your showcase by method of

presentation, then slides should be submitted in advance to your personal tutor first to be checked over and then he/she will look to submit them in advance to the EPA organisation.

The apprentice showcase will normally be completed BEFORE any other stages of the end-point assessment. The EPA assessor will grade and report upon the outcome of the showcase. Some EPA centres will not give any feedback until all assessments have been completed.

Let's look at exactly what you need to put in to your showcase. If you look at each section step by step then this will make the task of putting together your showcase easier. Make sure you cover EVERY outcome so that you maximise your chances of success. Remember that this EPA requires 100% pass mark so you need to cover **everything** in your showcase.

Key words / Command Verbs

Take note of the key-words used in each question. It is important to understand the key words so that you know what your EPA assessor will be looking for when they are marking your work. The key words at the start of each question are known as 'command verbs'. They tell you what to do. There is a list of command verbs an explanation at the end of this section.

For example:

'Describe the types of customer(s) you deal with within your job role'.

You might respond with something like:

'Most of our customers are wealthy business people. They are generally looking for the best deal they can get as they shop around a lot. Our products are so expensive, and customers often buy in bulk because they then sell on the products they buy from us online and they want to make the best possible profit they can. They are often so busy that they don't want to chat much, and they want to get straight to the point of the sale so that they can get on and do the next thing they need to do. Some customers are a bit more friendly and take the time to make conversation a bit more, but typically, my customers are very busy people'.

A response like:

'Busy, rich people' would be insufficient. This is because the command verb 'describe' has not been met.

Putting your showcase together.

First of all – decide which format you are going to use. You can produce a word document, PowerPoint, handwritten document or video. The format doesn't really matter, it is the content that matters. However, some EPA centres might have their own rules about how they want it presented so always check before you start work as you wouldn't want to waste your time making a video, for example, which the EPA organisation won't accept.

Secondly - make a start, write a header, or something, anything. Tasks are always more daunting before you make a start on them.

I personally like presentations (like PowerPoint slides). They are quick to put together, easy to edit and to add pictures to if you want to. It is also nice because you can move the order of the slides round easily to make the showcase flow better. That way, if you write it in a random order, at least you can make it flow correctly afterwards without hours of copy and paste. But the choice is yours. Word documents are great too.

The main thing is to get started. If you are using PowerPoint as a format for presenting your showcase, that's fine, but unless you want to actually present (as in deliver a presentation to go with the slides) then you will need to make sure ALL the information is on the slides. If you are going to physically present as well as use slides, then you should bullet point only.

Make a cover first for your showcase. It doesn't need to be too complicated but something to give your EPA assessor a good first impression of your work.

Something simple, like the one below will do. You can add a date, your job role and the company name as well if you want to.

The photo below shows an example cover for a showcase, created using PowerPoint.

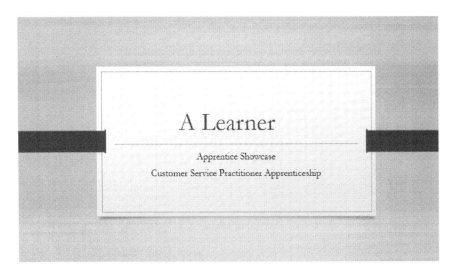

Ok, great, you have made a cover. It's a start and once you get started you might just get on a roll.

Now, pick a question that you already know the answer to. Write out the answer. It doesn't need to be in order, just yet, we need to get you on a roll.

Alternatively, you can work methodically from question 1 all the way to the end, whatever floats your boat! What you want to avoid though is stopping on a question if you find it a bit tricky. You can always contact your tutor for some support on anything you are struggling with.

To give you an idea of the standard of work, and detail, required, there is a sample answer shown below for you.

My Showcase

- I work as a customer service apprentice at Sales Are Us Ltd.
- Sales Are Us Ltd., sell spare parts for household appliances, like vacuum bags, door knobs for ovens, the glass shelves in fridges and so on.
- Its good because if you break something, you can probably repair it, things like washing machines, fridges and cookers are really expensive to replace so if you can repair them for a fraction of the cost, then this saves you lots of money.

Explain the difference between the features and benefits of products and/or services in relation to the organisation.

- So, the feature / benefit comparison would be this:

- Feature – spare parts to fix your appliance
- Benefit – saves you money so you can spend money on more interesting things than a new washing machine, such as that holiday you were saving for

- The features of a product are facts about it, so what it does, the benefits of a product are what it does for you or how it helps

Describe how to maintain knowledge of the organisation's products and/or services.

* I keep my knowledge up to date by:
* Attending training sessions each month on new products. This month was cooker door insert training, so we looked at how these work and how to sell them to customers
* I also check on the system each time I sell a product. I read out the product information to customers and so that helps me learn about which products are best when other customers call in and aren't sure what product they need
* I also look at the newsletter that comes round each day with new information on to help us with selling products to customers

As you can see, I have made it really clear to the EPA assessor which question I have answered by heading my slides with the question. That way, there is no doubt that I have answered it.

In the slide above I have given 3 different examples of ways in which I keep my knowledge of products up to date. This ensures that the marker, if they are not keen on my first answer, has others to consider and so I am confident I have covered everything in my answer and I will gain the marks needed to pass this element of the showcase.

Summary:

- Choose the format you are going to use for your showcase (PowerPoint/Word document)
- Get started & make a cover page to inspire you

- Begin working through each of the questions and requirements in each of the sections below
- Check you have answered every outcome and requirement against the assessment plan
- Show your manager/tutor/friend or anyone who has the patience to read and check it for you to look to see if you have missed anything
- Make sure your work is your own and your **answers relate to your own job role** and industry
- Never copy and paste from the internet. Assessors have clever ways of checking for this and your work is highly likely to be rejected if you do.

Knowledge questions to answer in your showcase.

There **are only 14 questions** including the distinction questions.

Give the distinction questions a try if you can. Then look at the behaviours you need to showcase afterwards.

SHOWCASE KNOWLEDGE QUESTIONS:

Prepare CLEAR AND DETAILED WRITTEN RESPONSES TO THE 14 QUESTIONS BELOW:
(UNLESS YOU ARE DOING AN ORAL PRESENATATION and in that case then prepare notes or presentation slides)

Tick off when done	The main question you need to answer is in this column	When you are putting your answer together, also look to answer these related questions. Answering these will help ensure you cover all areas of the question and don't miss anything.
1	Explain the use of different systems, equipment and/or technology available in the organisation to meet customer needs effectively	What are the systems, equipment and/or technology your organisation uses to effectively meet customer needs? In your role how would you use the systems, equipment and/or technology to support customer needs?
2	Describe the measures and evaluation tools used in the organisation to monitor customer service levels	What are the types of measurement used to monitor customer service levels? What are the types of evaluation tool used to monitor customer service levels?
3	State the aims of the organisation in relation to its sector AND state what is meant by the organisation's 'brand promise'	What is the difference between public, private and third sector organisation? What is your organisation business type and purpose? What does 'brand promise' mean?
4	Explain how the organisation's core values relate to its service culture	What is meant by an organisations core value? What are your organisations core values? What is meant by service culture? What is your

		organisations service culture? How does your organisations core values link to the service culture?
5	State the purpose of different organisational policies and procedures that affect their customer service role	What is the purpose of an organisational policy? List the organisational policies and procedures that could affect a customer service role. What should be included in a complaints process or procedure?
6	Describe the type of guidelines in a digital media policy that affect the use of social and digital media in the work environment.	What is meant by digital media? What digital media policies exist in customer service organisations?
7	OPTIONAL: DISTINCTION QUESTION: Explain how the organisational policies and procedures impact on the delivery of customer service	THIS IS A DISTINCTION QUESTION AND THERE IS NO ADDITIONAL GUIDANCE TO BREAK DOWN THE QUESTION
8	Explain how the relevant legislation and regulations affect the organisation's customer service provision	Identify appropriate legislation and regulation and how this effects your organisation.
9	State the responsibilities of employees and employers under the Health and Safety at Work Act	Why is it important to keep information confidential within an organisation? What information needs to be kept and remain confidential within your organisation? What are the responsibilities of

		the *employee* under the health and safety at work act? What are the responsibilities of the *employer* under the health and safety at work act?
10	OPTIONAL DISTINCTION QUESTION: Explain the potential impact on the organisation if it fails to adhere to each of the relevant legislation and regulations.	THIS IS A DISTINCTION QUESTION AND THERE IS NO ADDITIONAL GUIDANCE TO BREAK DOWN THE QUESTION
11	OPTIONAL DISTINCTION QUESTION: Explain how a code of practice or ethical standards affects customer service	THIS IS A DISTINCTION QUESTION AND THERE IS NO ADDITIONAL GUIDANCE TO BREAK DOWN THE QUESTION
12	Explain the difference between the features and benefits of products and/or services in relation to the organisation.	What are your organisations products and/or services? What is the difference between providing a product and providing a service?
13	Describe how to maintain your knowledge of the organisation's products and/or services.	How do you update and maintain your knowledge of your organisation's products and/or services?
14	OPTIONAL DISTINCTION QUESTION: Explain why it is important to update your knowledge of the organisation's products and/or services.	THIS IS A DISTINCTION QUESTION AND THERE IS NO ADDITIONAL

		GUIDANCE TO BREAK DOWN THE QUESTION

Tick off each of the number boxes to show that you have answered the questions.

Now let's look at the behaviours you need to show in the showcase.

In order to demonstrate your behaviours through your showcase you will need to produce evidence.

Have a discussion with your tutor about which evidence would be most suitable for your showcase. Some evidence ideas have been listed for you in the table below.

When you submit evidence for your showcase, please annotate it to show what it covers and the context the evidence came from.

Remember that your EPA assessor doesn't know your job role or procedures. You may think you're stating the obvious when you write what a piece of evidence is but it may not be obvious to an outsider to your company or industry.

	WHAT YOU NEED TO SHOW YOU HAVE DONE	**EVIDENCE IDEAS**
1	Identify customer needs: **Offer** appropriate product and/or service options to meet the identified needs of customers and the needs of the organisation.	CUSTOMER ORDER FORMS
2	Offer product and/or service options to customers in a logical and reasoned manner. Clearly explain how options offered meet the customer needs. **Communicate** to customers in a clear and coherent manner how the products and/or	FEEDBACK FROM CUSTOMERS, WITNESS REPORTS, REFLECTIVE ACCOUNT SIGNED BY MANAGER TO CONFIRM

	services meet their needs.	
3	Handle customer objections in a positive and professional manner. **Handle** customer objections in a positive and professional manner	FEEDBACK FROM CUSTOMERS, WITNESS REPORTS, REFLECTIVE ACCOUNT SIGNED BY MANAGER TO CONFIRM
4	**DISTINCTION: Provide** appropriate explanations to customers in situations where a mutually beneficial outcome cannot be reached.	FEEDBACK FROM CUSTOMERS, WITNESS REPORTS, REFLECTIVE ACCOUNT SIGNED BY MANAGER TO CONFIRM / CUSTOMER EMAILS / ACCOUNT NOTES
5	Agree goals and deadlines for completing tasks with an appropriate person. Prioritise and plan the completion of tasks to meet delivery deadlines. **Prioritise and plan** the completion of tasks according to agreed deadlines.	PERFORMANCE REVIEWS / TO DO LISTS / EMAILS SHOWING WORK COMPLETED ON TIME
6	Use tools and techniques to monitor progress of tasks. Monitor and adjust priorities as required. Meet agreed deadlines. **Use** appropriate tools and techniques to monitor the progress of tasks completion.	PERFORMANCE REVIEWS / TO DO LISTS EMAILS SHOWING WORK COMPLETED ON TIME
7	**DISTINCTION: Respond** in a professional manner to challenges and changes and adjust priorities accordingly.	PERFORMANCE REVIEWS / WITNESS REPORTS
8	Show patience, calmness and empathy when dealing with challenging customer situations. Use active listening skills when communicating with customers. Use appropriate questioning skills. **Maintain** calm and patience at all times when dealing with challenging customer situations.	WITNESS REPORTS / PERFOMANCE APPRAISALS / CUSTOMER FEEDBACK
9	Show understanding of the customer view point. **Demonstrate** sensitivity to, and interest in, the customers' concerns.	WITNESS REPORTS / PERFOMANCE APPRAISALS / CUSTOMER FEEDBACK / TRANSCRIPTS OF CUSTOMER CALLS
10	Explain the next steps and/or customer options in a logical manner. **Communicate** in a clear and coherent manner the next steps and/or options to meet the needs and expectations of customers.	WITNESS REPORTS / PERFOMANCE APPRAISALS / CUSTOMER FEEDBACK / TRANSCRIPTS OF CUSTOMER CALLS
11	Provide clear sign-posting or resolution to meet customers' needs and manage customer expectations. Deal with and resolve the customer conflict or challenge presented in line with	WITNESS REPORTS / PERFOMANCE APPRAISALS / CUSTOMER FEEDBACK / TRANSCRIPTS OF

	organisational and/or policies procedure.	CUSTOMER CALLS / NOTES ON CUSTOMER ACCOUNTS
12	Keep customers informed of progress while resolving issues.	WITNESS REPORTS / PERFOMANCE APPRAISALS / CUSTOMER FEEDBACK / TRANSCRIPTS OF CUSTOMER CALLS / NOTES ON CUSTOMER ACCOUNTS
13	**Maintain** accurate records of customer issues and progress to resolution	CUSTOMER ACCOUNT RECORDS / WITNESS REPORTS
14	DISTINCTION: **Take ownership** of customer issues, taking the appropriate actions to ensure customers' needs and expectations are met.	CUSTOMER ACCOUNT RECORDS / WITNESS REPORTS
15	**Identify** own strengths and weaknesses in relation to working within a customer service role. **Apply** the techniques of self-assessment to look at own strengths and weaknesses. **Conduct** a self-assessment to identify own strengths and weaknesses in relation to the job role.	SELF ASSESSMENT ACTIVITIES / ANALYSE OWN STRENGTHS, WEAKNESSES, OPPORTUNITES AND THREATS (SWOT ANALYSIS) PERFORMANCE REVIEWS
16	**Prepare a personal development plan** that helps to achieve personal goals and development needs. **Review and update** your personal development plan. The personal development plan should support the achievement of agreed learning and development goals.	PERSONAL DEVELOPMENT PLAN (LOOK FOR ONE ONLINE TO GIVE YOU IDEAS THEN ADAPT. UPDATE IT AS YOU GO THROUGH THE PROCESS).
17	DISTINCTION: Review the effectiveness of their personal development plan and update it accordingly.	PRODUCE A WRITTEN PIECE OF WORK REVIEWING YOUR PDP AND SHOW THE CHANGES YOU HAVE MADE AS A RESULT OF THE REVIEW.
18	Identify suitable ways of obtaining informal and formal feedback from others. Obtain useful and constructive feedback about your own service skills and knowledge from others. Seek constructive feedback about their customer service skills and knowledge from others	CUSTOMER FEEDBACK / ONLINE REVIEWS (THAT RELATE TO YOU DIRECTLY) / WITNESS REPORTS
19	Positively respond to all feedback. Use the feedback received to take responsibility for maintaining and developing your personal customer service skills and knowledge. Use feedback from others to develop own customer	PERFORMANCE APPRAISALS / WITNESS REPORTS / REFLECTIVE ACCOUNT

	service skills and knowledge.	
20	Demonstrate the interpersonal skills required to work effectively as part of a team. Work with others in a positive and productive manner.	EMAILS TO COLLEAGUES / MEETING MINUTES / WITNESS REPORTS
21	Communicate consistently with team members in the interest of helping customers. Demonstrate cooperation when working with others. Communicate information in a timely and reliable manner to team members to support them in meeting customer needs efficiently	EMAILS TO COLLEAGUES / MEETING MINUTES / WITNESS REPORTS / PERFORMANCE APPRAISAL
22	DISTINCTION: Recognise when to adapt personal behaviours and communication approach to meet the needs of team members and customers	EMAILS TO COLLEAGUES / MEETING MINUTES / WITNESS REPORTS / PERFORMANCE APPRAISAL
23	Share personal learning with others to support good practice. Present your ideas and recommendations for improvements in customer service to others.	EMAILS TO COLLEAGUES / MEETING MINUTES / WITNESS REPORTS / PERFORMANCE APPRAISAL / PROJECT WORK
24	DISTINCTION: Present reasoned ideas for improving customer service practice to the appropriate colleagues	EMAILS TO COLLEAGUES / MEETING MINUTES / WITNESS REPORTS / PERFORMANCE APPRAISAL / PROJECT WORK

EXAMPLE EVIDENCE

Below is a little more detail about some of the evidence types to help you prepare for your showcase. You should be used to gathering evidence by now. If you have any queries, have a chat with your personal tutor.

Witness reports	*Show your manager the table of information above. Ask him/her to write a statement to show how you have met each criteria, giving examples of how you have done it.*
Performance appraisals	*You should get plenty of feedback as an apprentice and some of this*

	should be documented. You might be able to use it to meet the criteria above. Read it through, photocopy and highlight which areas you think it could meet for you.
Emails	Emails are great evidence of you dealing with customers and can show the good work you have done. You should add some notes to emails to give some context to the email so that your EPA assessor understands what you did
Meeting minutes	These are only useful if you are directly mentioned in them and they clearly state how you have met the criteria.
Customer feedback	You can either create your own feedback survey or collect ones your company already use. Have a look to see which criteria they meet.

Have a look at the piece of evidence shown below.

This is a letter from a customer thanking a customer service practitioner (in this case, James) for his help.

Which of the criteria above do you think a piece of evidence like this could help James with if he was to use it in his showcase?

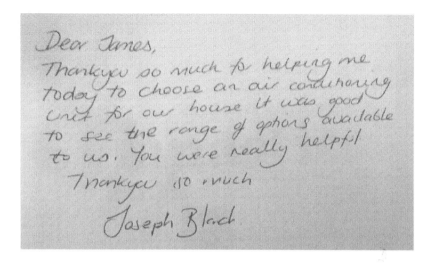

Dear James,

Thankyou so much for helping me today to choose an air conditioning unit for our house it was good to see the range of options available to us. You were really helpful

Thankyou so much

Joseph Black

So, this meets outcome 1 as it shows that James clearly identified the customer needs. Also 2 has been met as James showed the customer a range of options and the customer was happy about it. Outcome 2 has been met because James showed a range of options. Outcome 3 has not been met because the letter does not show that James overcame any objections.

If you are using evidence of this type, then try to authenticate it. Essentially, anyone could write a letter like this, and so to show it is genuine, you could attach a copy of a receipt to show what the customer ordered or ask your manager to sign it as a witness.

Don't worry if your evidence is not 'perfect' looking. Naturally occurring evidence won't be perfect. Like the letter above, it may not be professionally produced, and a lot of customer feedback might be on a note, or a thankyou card. It doesn't mean you can't use it. Authenticity of evidence is important, so you might need to add notes to explain the context behind the evidence.

Other excellent sources of evidence are feedback forms filled in by customers, or social media review (e.g. Facebook, trip advisor), but to use these they would have to specifically mention your name.

A good idea would be to create a customer survey (if your company don't use these already). You can then use this as evidence to show you have met the criteria. Surveys are easy to create using Microsoft Word. Simply go into Word, click 'file' and then 'new'. You will then see this screen:

Then simply type the word 'survey' and you will be given options as to which type of survey you want to use. You can then word the questions you want to ask your customers to suit the requirements of your showcase. Then simply hand out to customers and once you have responses, you can take photos and upload them to your showcase document. An example customer survey, created on a word document is on the next page.

Systems and versions of Microsoft Word can vary, so have a look online for instructions if you are not sure or if your system works differently.

[Company Name]

How are we doing?

We are committed to providing you with the best dining experience possible, so we welcome your comments. Please fill out this questionnaire and place it in the box in our lobby. Thank you.

Please rate the quality of the service you received from your server

☐ 1 ☐ 2 ☐ 3 ☐ 4 ☐ 5

Disappointing   Exceptional

How well did your server identify and meet your needs?

☐ 1 ☐ 2 ☐ 3 ☐ 4 ☐ 5

Disappointing   Exceptional

Please rate the quality of your entree.

☐ 1 ☐ 2 ☐ 3 ☐ 4 ☐ 5

Disappointing   Exceptional

Were you offered a range of services or alternative products?

☐ 1 ☐ 2 ☐ 3 ☐ 4 ☐ 5

Disappointing   Exceptional

How sell did your server listen to your needs and meet your expectations?

☐ 1 ☐ 2 ☐ 3 ☐ 4 ☐ 5

Disappointing   Exceptional

Please rate your overall dining experience.

☐ 1 ☐ 2 ☐ 3 ☐ 4 ☐ 5

Disappointing   Exceptional

What was the name of your server?   /   Customer name/date/signature

---

Example witness statement:

Have a look to see which of the criteria you think this witness statement meets.

FAO End Point Assessment Organisation

From Dan Charles, Team Leader at XDN Group.

Telephone: xxxxxx   Email <u>Dan.charles@xdngroup.co.uk</u>

Regarding – Paul Warner – Customer Service Practitioner Apprentice.

Paul has worked within my team as a customer service apprentice for the past 12 months. Paul works in the call centre, dealing with customer requests to book in engineers to repair household appliances, such as cookers or fridges.

Paul knows to prioritise the phone lines, as if we don't answer timely then we lose business. In between calls, Paul makes sure that he follows up any complicated customer queries or sends in reports we have asked for.

Paul is consistent at sending in reports on time and he keeps a spreadsheet to record all the bookings and payments he has made each day. He also keeps a to-do list, which helps him to keep track of his tasks for the day and he shows me this and lets me know if there are any tasks remaining, for example, if he is waiting news from another department and so has to follow up the next day. Paul is an excellent and valued member of the team and has a fantastic rapport with customers. He often looks to sell additional services to customers, such as insurance products.

Top tips when asking for witness statements:

- Ask the witness to look at the assessment plan (or the list of criteria above) so they know exactly what the EPA assessor will be looking for

- Make sure it gives their contact details for authenticity (full name, job title, relationship to you as the apprentice & phone number)
- Ask the witness to give examples of what you do in your day to day tasks
- Use the assessment plan (and/or list above) yourself to tick off exactly what the witness testimony meets so that you know what other criteria you will need to meet from other evidence.
- Show your tutor and ask them for feedback and see if they agree with the criteria you think it meets.
- Offer to make the witness a cup of tea or coffee while they write it, managers can be very busy people, let them see that you might be saving them time!

Other ideas:

- Take a photo of your to-do list or system scheduler.
- screen shot customer service entries on system.
- Always check that you are permitted to use evidence and you are not breaking any data protection rules or GDPR guidance.

Checking and proof-reading your work

Once you are confident that your answers make sense and you have met all of the criteria, then spellcheck/grammar check your work. If you have used a word document to prepare your showcase, you could even listen to it to make certain that it flows ok. To do this, in a word document, click 'view', then click 'read mode', then click 'view' again, and 'read aloud'. There will then be a 'play' icon at the upper right-hand side of the screen. Different versions of Word may vary the commands, so just Google it if you have any issues. This is a great new tool for proof-reading and checking your own work.

Put your work away for a day or so and then check it over with fresh eyes. The pass and distinction criteria are a bit like the mark scheme, so you can see exactly what the EPA assessor will be marking your work against, by reviewing the criteria. Reflect on your own work yourself, it was someone else's work and you were marking it, would you realistically award the mark? This will give you a good idea of how you will do when your work is marked and give you a good basis on which to make any changes before you hand it in.

Next, go to the website which shows the assessment plan for your apprenticeship standard which is shown below. Check that your showcase meets all the requirements and that you have not missed anything.

https://www.instituteforapprenticeships.org/media/1166/customer_service_practitioner.pdf

If you are planning on verbally presenting your presentation slides to the EPA assessor, then you will need to practice this. You could practice the delivery of your showcase to colleagues, friends, your tutor or your manager. You could even practice it alone. If you are really confident, you could video record or voice record your presentation and watch it to give yourself ideas on how to improve when it comes to the real thing. You will need to send your presentation slides into the EPA in advance and arrange a date/time for the live presentation. Specifics of how this will be arranged can vary between EPA centres and how they chose to organise assessments, so please check with them or ask your personal tutor to make enquiries for you.

If you are now happy with your showcase then show it to your tutor/assessor to look over. They will then liaise with the EPA organisation in order to get this submitted and marked for you.

Most EPA organisations will get the results over to you within around 14 working days, but service levels vary between organisations, so if in doubt, ask your tutor or contact your EPA organisation.

Once the showcase has been submitted you can now look at preparing for the next two stages of your EPA.

Apprentice showcase key features:

- This is the first thing the EPA assessor will see and will use this to 'get to know you and your skills/knowledge

- Can be showcased through delivery of a presentation or by a virtual form of assessment such as a report, storyboard or journal or word document
- Weighted at 65% of the EPA
- A chance to show off skills and the application of knowledge
- 100% of all the pass criteria to achieve a pass
- 100 % of the pass criteria PLUS 70% of the distinction criteria to achieve a distinction.
- Remember to add lots of evidence to demonstrate the fantastic work you have done whilst on your apprenticeship
- Attempt every single outcome. Do not miss one out, it is 100% pass mark, double and triple check that you have covered everything you need to
- Attempt all of the distinction criteria if you can

Top Tips:

- Make your showcase short – about 12-15 pages long – but full of excellent evidence
- Some EPA centres will have specific rules about how long it should be, some don't
- Read, read and read again the assessment plan, then take it to your manager to read and ask him/her to write a detailed witness statement about your work and how you have met the standards
- Make sure not to miss out any of the criteria needed

- Use customer feedback surveys or similar evidence
- Check you have met the command verbs when answering questions (command verbs are the words at the start of questions that tell you what to do)

Use of command verbs

When you are putting together your showcase, take into consideration the command verbs below:

Command Verb	Requirement
Explain	Clarify a topic by giving a detailed account as to how and why it occurs, or what is meant by the use of this term in a particular context. The writing should have clarity so that complex procedures or sequences of events can be understood, defining key terms where appropriate, and be substantiated with relevant research. This should be sentences rather than bullet points.
Describe	Provide a detailed explanation as to how or why something happens. This should be sentences rather than bullet points. It should be clear that you understand the topic.
State	To specify in clear terms the key aspects pertaining to a topic without being overly descriptive. Refer to evidence and examples where appropriate. This can be a list rather than full sentences.
Offer	This is a behavioural command verb for which evidence should be seen to confirm that an offer has been made to the customer in the appropriate context

List	A simple list, does not have to be a written sentence and bullet points are acceptable
Communicate	This is a behavioural command verb for which evidence should be seen to confirm that suitable communication has been achieved.
Handle	This is a behavioural command verb and suitable evidence should be seen to show that the apprentice has been able to deal with (handle) the situation appropriately. It should be clear as to the context of the situation.
Demonstrate	This is a behavioural command verb and apprentices' work should show that a particular aspect has been seen
Conduct	This is a behavioural command verb and suitable evidence should be seen to show that the apprentice's behaviour is appropriate.
General Behavioural Questions	Any questions that require you to demonstrate skills/competencies and behaviours must be met with suitable evidence that is reliable, valid and sufficient to show competence in this area. This could be evidenced by: - Work-based product evidence - Video evidence - Learning journals (for feedback section) - Performance appraisals - Other suitable evidence

This is a guide only and should be used to help you prepare for your End Point Assessment. It is HIGHLY recommended that you read the assessment plan for this apprenticeship standard, which can be found online. Also, please check the criteria and information sent to you by the EPA centre you will be assessed by.

https://www.instituteforapprenticeships.org/apprenticeship-standards/customer-service-practitioner/

9 EPA OBSERVATION

Your observation is one of the most important parts of your EPA. This is when you get the chance to show off your newly honed customer service skills in a real-life working environment.

You should be used to being observed now as your own personal tutor/assessor will have observed you and produced observation reports to use as evidence towards your on programme learning and for any formal qualifications that are built in to your apprenticeship.

Practical observation grade summary / overview
Pass = 100%
Distinction = All of the pass criteria plus 80% of the distinction criteria
Weighted at 20% of the EPA
The observation will last one hour

The timing of your observation is essential. You need to book your observation, if possible, on a time and day that will allow you to show off your skills to the best of your ability.

Have a think about when this is likely to be. If you book in the observation for a quiet time, there may not be enough customers for you to serve to showcase your skills. Alternatively, if you book it for a busy time, then you might be so busy that you don't give as good service to some customers than you would normally and so this would not show you at your best either.

An even worse situation would be if there were no customers, as you can't show customer service skills when there is no one to service!

I have known customer service apprentices who work in high end sales, so one sale a week would be a good result for them and customers are few and far between, but when they do come in they spend an awful lot of money, so it still makes sense for the company to hire them. If you are in a situation like this you really do need to think long and hard about the timing for your observation and see if you can book customer appointments in to coincide with your EPA observation.

Once you have identified the perfect time for your observation and booked a time that best suits (if you can) you need to look at what the observation will involve. The more you know about what the observer is looking for, the more you are likely to get a great result.

The observation will be conducted at your normal place of work and can be done when you are dealing with customers either:

- Face to face
- By telephone
- Online
- OR other customer service in line with the assessment plan

The main purpose of the observation is for the end point assessor to be able to see your use of:
- Communication skills
- Interpersonal skills
- Suitable behaviours
- Managing customers' needs and expectations
- Dealing with general customer interactions and requests

The EPA assessor will create an observation report, documenting what has been seen during the practical observation. Alternatively, they may video record it and use a checklist.

The EPA assessor will then mark this against the

criteria to ensure that all required areas are covered where possible.

The EPA assessor might handwrite, type, video or audio record the observation report. They will probably discuss the method of recording the observation with you in advance, particularly if they are looking to record it on video or voice recording. If the EPA assessor wants to video you, you have the right to refuse this. But don't worry too much, it's not like they will put it on YouTube or anything! The EPA assessor is duty bound to keep your information and recordings secure and only available for viewing by those authorised to do so, such as auditors and others that check the quality of their work.

The EPA assessor will want to observe you with at least two customers if possible, so as discussed earlier, make sure you have plenty of customers to work with when the assessor is with you.

The assessment plan for your apprenticeship does allow for remote observation. This means that the EPA assessor could observe you via Skype or other real-time video-based technology. This might be a good option for you if you are nervous. From an assessor point of view, this is quite difficult to organise and most EPA centres will not offer remote observations, but it is something worth considering if you really don't want the assessor in the room with you.

The observation will normally last around an hour. Even if your assessor sees you do everything they need to do early in the observation, they may still observe you for the full hour. If the assessor doesn't see everything in the hour, they may stay a little longer, say up to an hour and a half.

Where evidence cannot be observed directly during the practical observation element of the EPA, the EPA assessor can use alternative methods to gather suitable evidence, such as

- Work based product evidence
- Witness reports

The alternative evidence can only be used in exceptional circumstances and not for all elements of the standard are suitable for alternative evidence. Your own EPA assessor will ask you for any alternative evidence they need and each EPA centre will have their own guidelines on what is acceptable.

TIP:

Be nice to your EPA assessor, they may have travelled a long way. Offer them a drink and be friendly. Try having a chat with them about how their journey was and build up a rapport.

This shows that you are using your customer service skills with visitors to your place of work and gives your assessor a good first impression of you as a customer service practitioner. It may help you to relax too.

So, what exactly do you need to show in your

observation? Look at the criteria in the table below.

PLEASE NOTE DISTINCTION CRITERIA ARE IN ITALICS

Skills and competencies	Pass/*Distinction* Criteria
Demonstrate effective interpersonal skills that achieve positive customer engagement using: - Effective use of open and closed questioning skills relevant to the situation - Effective use of active listening skills when communicating - Effective use of body language when interacting with customers - Working with others and sharing good practice when performing your duties -	Demonstrate willingness and ability to engage with customers in a positive manner using relevant interpersonal skills.
Distinction	*Demonstrate ability to adapt interpersonal skills when working on meeting the needs and expectations of different customers, showing knowledge of the application of the Equality Act when communicating (verbally or non-verbally).*
Recognise customer needs and expectations Respond to customer needs and manage expectations in a professional and timely manner	Work with customers to build a rapport, recognising and where possible meeting their needs and expectations.
Distinction	*Demonstrate ability to balance the needs and expectations of the customer with that of the organisation*
Build and maintain a rapport	Show willingness to work with others and share ideas

with customers	where appropriate.
Distinction criteria	*Pro-actively work with others to ensure efficient customer service delivery.*
Use appropriate methods of verbal and non-verbal communication skills relevant to your work environment	Demonstrate ability to make initial customer contact and use appropriate verbal and non-verbal communication skills
Use appropriate body language to maintain or enhance the customer experience	Adapt tone, behaviour and body language when necessary, recognising and confirming understanding of needs and expectations.
Adapt the tone and/or behaviour to maintain or enhance the customer experience as appropriate	Demonstrate ability to recognise when to summarise and the techniques to use.
Distinction *Assessors can take into consideration the job role and adapt to suit for some outcomes*	*In all roles: Demonstrate ability to adapt communication - tone, behaviour and language - to different customers and their interactions, showing clear knowledge of the application of the Equality Act in all customer handing.*
Distinction	*In all roles: Demonstrate ability to flex to various customer personalities, while remaining calm and in control where necessary. They will also demonstrate they know the organisational procedures to be followed in all communication and the importance to the brand/organisation of this requirement*
Confirm yours, and the customers, understanding of the customer's needs and expectations	Non- facing'. Demonstrate ability to make initial customer contact and make use of appropriate communication skills.
Use summarising language and/or reinforcement techniques during customer interaction to confirm understanding.	Adapts tone and behaviour when necessary, recognising and confirming understanding of needs and expectations.
Use correct, appropriate and clear communication skills e.g. written and verbal that reflect your organisations brand	Demonstrates ability to recognise and use reinforcement techniques during customer interactions

Treat all customers equally, ensuring that you comply with legal requirements Recognise and respond to individual needs to provide a personalised customer service experience	Recognise and respond to individual needs to provide a personalised customer service experience
Act in a way that upholds the core values and service culture of the organisation	Behave in a way that upholds the core values and service culture of the organisation.
Present a tidy and professional image Know and follow organisational dress code Be approachable and welcoming when dealing with customers face to face	Present a professional image in line with the organisational dress code and code of conduct.
Use a welcoming and approachable tone when in non-face to face situations Present a positive attitude with all customers and in various situations	Demonstrate a positive attitude and welcoming approach consistently when dealing with customers.
Maintain professional and positive language in all situations Be confident and calm in difficult situations	Maintain professional and positive language consistently in customer interactions.
Make initial approach to customers in professional manner following organisational procedures	Demonstrate ability to confidently approach customers, remaining positive and professional when circumstances are challenging.

Establish customer needs from customer wants Work towards meeting customer needs Adapt tone and behaviour to meet customer needs and expectations	They will show an ability to establish needs and expectations, working towards meeting them where possible, explaining when necessary when they cannot be met
Recognise customer expectations Manage customer expectations Check customer satisfaction Remain positive and professional when explaining when customer needs and/or expectations cannot be met.	Demonstrate knowledge of the organisational products and/or services and knowledge and application of the organisation's policies and procedures.
Establish initial contact with customers Recognise customer wants, needs and expectations	Demonstrate recognition of own role, responsibilities, level of authority and organisational procedures when dealing with customers.
Take responsibility and work with customers to achieve outcome. Maintain contact with customers where necessary and as promised (even if no additional information is available)	Take ownership from beginning to end, building and maintaining a relationship with the customer
Refer customers to others as required accurately passing on necessary information Follow up as required to ensure outcome is reached Follow up as required to ensure outcome is reached. Following organisational procedures, check customer satisfaction	Recognise the importance of good customer service to the customer and in turn the organisation, making contact as promised, referring to others as necessary with all required detail, following up to ensure conclusion.

Top tips to prepare for your observation

- Observe your colleague or manager at work serving customers
- Video or audio record yourself dealing with customers then mark your performance against the checklist above
- Ask your tutor if they can arrange for a mock observation
- Ask your manager to observe you using the checklist and feedback to you to see how you got on
- Don't worry too much if you don't have the opportunity to show off all your skills on the day. Remember you will already have showcased your work and you will have a discussion with your EPA assessor which may give you another opportunity to meet the criteria
- When you are out shopping or using other customer service facilities, have a think about the service you receive. Would the server meet all the requirements on the checklist?

10 EPA PROFESSIONAL DISCUSSION

The professional discussion is the final area of the EPA.

Professional discussion grade summary

Pass = 100%

Distinction = All the pass criteria, plus 75% of the distinction criteria

Weighted at 15% of the EPA

The discussion will last around one hour.

The best form of preparation for the professional discussion is practice. Below there is a list of questions that you MAY be asked. You MIGHT NOT be asked the exact questions but they will give you a very good idea of what to expect. EPA assessors will adapt the questions they use but they will all need to meet the same criteria (look in the assessment plan again).

Your EPA assessor will have already reviewed your showcase and completed your observation so they will have a very good idea of what you are like as a customer service practitioner and what your skills are. They will also be looking to 'fill gaps' in the evidence you have produced for them so far. The EPA assessor will be looking for reasons TO pass you, not reasons to fail you. This is a good opportunity to fill those gaps and make sure you gain as many marks as you possibly can.

The more you practice this discussion, the less nervous you will be on the day and therefore the better you are likely to perform. Practice with your colleagues, partners, family, friends, the dog/cat/goldfish or whoever/whatever is willing to listen to you. Ok, maybe the goldfish won't give you feedback, but at least it won't interrupt you!!

Ask your tutor if he or she can arrange a mock discussion for you.

Example questions:

- Tell me about your customers – who are they? - Who are your organisations' customers? - Please can you describe the different types of customers - What is an internal customer? - What is an external customer? - Who are your organisations internal customers? - Who are your organisations external customers? - What is the difference between internal and external customers to the organisation? DISTINCTION QUESTIONS - D1 Explain the importance of building good customer relationships to the organisation. - D2 Explain the difference in the way internal and external relationships are managed.	**Make notes here**

- What is the purpose of customer service? - What are the different needs of your customers? What customers have specific needs? - What are the different priorities of your customers? - What do you understand by equality law? - Can you describe the specific needs of different customers, including those protected under equality law? - What is meant by customer expectations? - How does the standard of customer service affect the success of your organisation? - When do you adapt your service approach to meet the needs and expectations of your customers - How do you adapt your service approach to meet the needs and expectations of your customers? DISTINCTION QUESTION: - D3 Explain the importance of balancing the needs of both the organisation and its customers.	

- Tell me about your job role and your responsibilities. - How do your actions impact on others in your organisation? - What targets and goals do you work to within your job role? - How do you achieve these targets and goals?	

- What is meant by a customer focused experience? - How do you establish the facts to create a customer focused experience? - How do you use the facts to create an appropriate response? - Why is building customer trust important? - How would you start to build trust with your customers? For DISTINCTION - D4 Explain how to respond to customer needs and requirements positively.	

11 EPA COSTINGS

The training provider or college you have been training with, in conjunction with your employer, will be responsible for funding the EPA.

You should not be asked for any money to complete your EPA.

The amount companies can charge the employer or training provider for EPA depends on the amount of funding for the standard and the EPA maximum chargeable rate is calculated as a percentage of this.

Typical costs for an EPA for the Customer Service Practitioner vary between around £450 to £600.

The structure of the EPA, with three elements, means that EPA companies will not be making substantial profits on your EPA. If you bear in mind the office facilities, assessor costs, training, administrative costs and travel, it really is not that much money for the EPA company to assess you for.

Re-sits are chargeable as well, but most EPA

centres will offer a price per element of the EPA that requires re-sit, so you will only have to retake the element(s) of the assessment you didn't pass first time.

This helps to keep costs lower for re-sits and you will need to find out how much the EPA re-sit will cost your employer if you find yourself in the re-take situation. However, if you have planned effectively and followed the hints and tips in this book, then you should, all being well, pass first time with flying colours.

12 RESITS

The rules around re-sits are designed by the EPA organisation with whom you are taking your EPA, who will follow guidance from the apprenticeship standard and the assessment plan.

Normally you will be permitted two re-sits. So, in effect, this means you get three chances at your EPA.

Not only that, if you work methodically through the three elements of your EPA then you can check that you have passed an element before moving onto the next.

This works particularly well with the apprentice showcase. You need to send this over to the EPA assessor first. There is little point putting yourself through an observation and professional discussion if you have not passed your showcase.

So, get your showcase handed in nice and early and see if you can get feedback on it. Your EPA assessor may not be able to tell you that you have passed this section. This is because the assessor will mark your showcase and give you a grade, but after that it will need to go for internal verification (basically this is where the work of the assessor is checked and approved). The EPA assessor will not be able to give you formal feedback until this checking process and any other checking, such as moderation, has been carried out.

That said, the EPA organisation shouldn't take too long to get your formal result to you.

The EPA organisation should be able to give you specific feedback if you have not passed your apprentice showcase, that way you can use the feedback to make suitable improvements before re-sending the showcase document. You will normally not be permitted to resubmit to increase your grade.

Next will be the observation. If you have followed the hints and tips in the relevant section of this book about the observation, you shouldn't have too many issues.

The observation, like all elements of the EPA can be re-taken. However, you may find that this is the most costly element of the EPA to re-sit, so your employer might not be very pleased if you need to re-sit.

The professional discussion can often 'mop up' any areas of the observation that the EPA assessor was not confident you had met or they want further information on. You might find that your professional discussion is conducted straight after your observation. Your EPA assessor might ask you questions about things that they would like to have seen in the observation but didn't quite work out or the opportunity to see it wasn't there on the day. Make the most of your professional discussion to give lots of real-life examples of things you have done with customers that cover it instead, this could save you a re-sit if you convince your assessor that you are competent and should pass, even if they have not quite seen all they would have liked.

You have (normally) three chances to pass your EPA and if you need to take all three then do so. Don't worry about what anyone else around you get, or what they think, just don't give up. Years after you have completed this apprenticeship, and years after you have lost touch with the majority of people you work with, you need as much evidence of success on your CV as you can. Show resilience, keep trying. Hopefully you won't need to re-sit, but if you do, don't get down about it, but make the most of the feedback you have been given by your EPA assessor, research, work harder and achieve the success you are looking for.

Don't forget your tutor is there to support you too and should offer you additional training and support sessions to support with any required re-sits. Your tutor will want you to pass your EPA as this is a reflection on their teaching, learning and preparation skills. Don't shy away from your tutor if you haven't passed. They will have seen others in the same situation and they won't judge you. Make time as soon as you can to get some support sessions booked with your tutor and get that re-sit booked in while information is still fresh in your mind.

13 PROGRESSION FOLLOWING YOUR APPRENTICESHIP COMPLETION

Once you have passed your apprenticeship Customer Service Practitioner, there are an array of progression possibilities.

The most of obvious progression route is to go on to the Level 3 Customer Service apprenticeship. There is a substantial 'jump' between levels and the level 3 will stretch and challenge students much more than the level 2. That said, the current level 3 customer service apprenticeship has not been released on a standard yet, so is coursework based.

You will need to pass your functional skills maths and English at level 2 to achieve the level 3 customer service apprenticeship if you have not done so already, but you can still progress to start the course without these (check admissions criteria).

If you now have more responsibility in your job role and you have others that you supervise, you could consider a team leading apprenticeship.

Alternatively, customer service and business administration tend to go hand in hand quite well, and you could look at a business administration level 2 or level 3 qualification.

Other options, depending on your job role, include sales, retail, trade supplier, business improvement techniques, marketing, recruitment or management apprenticeships.

If you are offered a progression route with your training provider, this is most likely because you have demonstrated that you are a good student and you are capable of working at the higher level they are offering you. Not all students will be offered progression, so if you are, then you should be proud that you have been selected, and if possible, you should make the most of opportunities that have been offered to you.

Completion of this apprenticeship will lead to eligibility to join the institute of Customer Service as an individual at professional level. Their website is detailed below:

https://www.instituteofcustomerservice.com/

14 FEEDBACK TO THE END POINT ASSESSMENT ORGANISATON

The end point assessment organisation should ask for your feedback following your experience with them.

It is important that you are open and honest in the feedback you give. End point assessment is new to centres, apprentices as well as end point assessment organisations. Therefore, the processes and procedures are very new and those in charge will be open to feedback and keen to change things to make apprentices feel more at ease.

If your EPA assessor or organisation don't ask for your feedback directly, you can always email them or look in their website for contact details.

15 THE CUSTOMER SERVICE PRACTITIONER STANDARD

The standard has been written by employer groups. The Customer Service Practitioner Level 2 Standard is designed to replace the Customer Service Level 2 Apprenticeship Framework. The old apprenticeship frameworks are still available (at time of print). However, these are being phased out and the new standard qualifications, like this one, are replacing them.

All apprentices need to meet the requirements of the standard to pass the EPA. The details of the standard can be found in full on the website below, where you can view the standard document in full.

You can view this document in full at:

https://www.instituteforapprenticeships.org/apprenticeship-standards/customer-service-practitioner/

This is an important document for you. Please take the time to read through it and that you view it online to ensure that you see any version updates.

The standard should be read in conjunction with the assessment plan. Please get to know these two documents, as they will ensure you have a thorough understanding of your apprenticeship and the requirements for your EPA.

16 THE CUSTOMER SERVICE PRACTITIONER ASSESSMENT PLAN

The assessment plan for Customer Service Practitioner sets out the requirements and processes for the end point assessment of this apprenticeship.

The assessment plan and the standard should be read in conjunction with each other.

The assessment plan is available online, and is one of the most important documents in relation to your apprenticeship.

It is well worth taking the time to read through the assessment plan as this will help you to learn exactly what your EPA assessor is looking for, as this forms the basis of any assessment work they will conduct with you.

You can find the full assessment plan document on line at:

https://www.instituteforapprenticeships.org/media/1166/customer_service_practitioner.pdf

It is highly recommended that you go online and read the assessment plan and the standard. There may be updates, so please always check online for the latest version.

17 APPEALING THE OUTCOME OF YOUR END POINT ASSESSMENT

In the (now hopefully unlikely) event that you don't pass your end point assessment or achieve the grade you want, you do have the right to appeal.

All EPA centres will have an appeals process. This should be available to you on their website, or on their e-file or paper file. If you can't get hold of the appeals process easily, then you can use the contact details on the EPA centre website to get hold of someone at the centre who can help you.

In the first instance, have a chat with your personal tutor, they may be able to support you in having your work re-marked by the EPA centre. If your own tutor can't help, then you can take matters into your own hands and go direct to the EPA centre. You need to be confident of why you think you should have received a better grade than you have. So always check over the assessment plan and have a look yourself to see if your work meets the criteria for the pass or distinction you are striving for. You might find that you have missed something important and that there is good reason for the grade you have been awarded and that once you have a good understanding of why you have been awarded the grade you have, you might find that you agree with them. At least by looking through the assessment plan and your work, you will gain a good insight into where you may have gone wrong.

If you still feel you want to appeal, then you need to go through the correct channels.

Once you have obtained a copy of the appeals procedure for the EPA centre, you can follow their processes to lodge your appeal. It might be easier if you call the EPA centre and ask to speak to the internal verifier who has checked the assessment work produced by your EPA assessor. This will be more likely to get your work looked at quickly, or they might ask you to complete a formal appeal request form.

The appeal will then be assessed and the EPA centre will have a certain amount of days to respond formally to your appeal. They should respond in writing and many centres will look to resolve your appeal within 14 working days but check their service levels with the centre directly.

If you are still not happy with the outcome of your appeal, you may be able to appeal to Ofqual (the Office of Qualifications and Examinations

Regulation), who are responsible for the external quality assurance for this qualification. However, this really should be the last resort.

The Ofqual website is shown below:

https://www.gov.uk/government/organisations/ofqual

The Ofqual complaints information page is also available on their website:

https://www.gov.uk/government/organisations/ofqual/about/complaints-procedure

Ofqual aim to complete all investigations as quickly as possible, and to complete 80% of cases within 40 working days. Some cases can be more complex and them longer to gather enough information to make a fair decision. Where their investigations take longer, they will keep you informed of progress on your case at least every 30 working days.

You can contact Ofqual by emailing complaints@ofqual.gov.uk or calling 0300 303 3346

Please make sure that you have exhausted the EPA centres own appeals procedures BEFORE you consider contacting Ofqual.

18 USEFUL WEBSITES FOR FURTHER INFORMATION

ACAS Employment Rights Helpline
http://www.acas.org.uk/index.aspx?articleid=4489

All about school leavers
https://www.allaboutschoolleavers.co.uk/articles/article/235/how-to-find-a-list-of-all-the-apprenticeships-available

Amazing Apprenticeships
https://twitter.com/AmazingAppsUK

Apprenticeship EPA Centre

www.apprenticeship-centre.co.uk/EPA or
Telephone 0845 22 5020 email
info@apprenticeship-centre.co.uk

Apprenticeship Helpline
Nationalhelpdesk@apprenticeships.gov.uk or
Telephone 0800 015 0400

Apprenticeships in Wales
http://gov.wales/topics/educationandskills/skillsandtraining/apprenticeships/?lang=en

BKSB Functional Skills Online Training
https://www.bksb.co.uk/

Customer Service Practitioner assessment plan
https://www.instituteforapprenticeships.org/media/1166/customer_service_practitioner.pdf

Customer Service Practitioner apprenticeship standard
https://www.instituteforapprenticeships.org/apprenticeship-standards/customer-service-practitioner/

ESFA
https://www.gov.uk/government/organisations/education-and-skills-funding-agency

ForSkills Functional Skills Online Training
http://www.forskills.co.uk/

Further Education and Skills Apprenticeships
https://www.gov.uk/topic/further-education-skills/apprenticeships

Get in, Go Far Government Apprenticeship Website
https://www.getingofar.gov.uk/

Institute of Customer Services
https://www.instituteofcustomerservice.com/

National Apprenticeship Service
https://www.gov.uk/apply-apprenticeship

Pearson Past Papers for Functional Skills

http://qualifications.pearson.com/en/support/support-topics/exams/past-papers.html

Prospects career advice

https://www.prospects.ac.uk/

Register of Apprenticeship Training Providers
https://www.gov.uk/guidance/register-of-apprenticeship-training-providers

The Apprenticeship Centre Facebook Page
https://www.facebook.com/TheApprenticeshipCentreBirmingham/

The Apprenticeship Centre
http://www.apprenticeship-centre.co.uk/

The Apprenticeship Levy
https://www.gov.uk/government/publications/apprenticeship-levy-how-it-will-work/apprenticeship-levy-how-it-will-work

The Ask Project
https://amazingapprenticeships.com/

The Institute for Apprenticeships
https://www.instituteforapprenticeships.org/

19 ABOUT THE AUTHOR

Louise Webber studied Psychology and Philosophy at The University of Liverpool. She then went on to study Management at Postgraduate Level.

Louise worked for three major banking institutions at management level and was very successful at meeting targets and audit requirements.

Louise went on to work in the education sector, working in both mainstream and special needs schools. She re-trained to work within the adult education sector and studied to become a tutor/assessor for NVQ and Apprenticeships then becoming Lead Internal Verifier within a training centre. Louise now works as Head of Apprenticeships and Head of End Point Assessment, responsible for the success of the Apprenticeship schemes, staff training and development, recruitment and quality management as well as being the Ofsted nominee for the centre.

Louise successfully applied via the tender process in 2018 for registration for her centre for status as an End Point Assessment Organisation who are registered on the Register of End Point Assessment Organisations (RoEPAO) as Apprenticeship EPA Centre.

Louise manages a team of End Point Assessors, internally verifies work and ensures processes and procedures are in place to meet the requirements of audit and compliance.

Louise has supported her team of tutors to successfully complete over 2000 Apprenticeship and NVQ courses for learners within the training centre where she works. In addition, Louise has worked as a Standards Verifier for the world's largest examination board, supporting other centres to achieve high standards for learners and success within the education sector.

Apprenticeship EPA Centre can be contacted on 0845 223 5020.

www.apprenticeship-centre.co.uk/epa

Louise has also worked with other end point assessment centres to support apprentices in preparation for their EPA and has written examination material for Apprenticeship EPA Centre.

Louise is the author of a guide book for those

interested in (or already on) apprenticeship courses:

'Apprenticeships: A Guide for Students and Parents', written in 2018 and also available on Amazon:

https://www.amazon.co.uk/Apprenticeships-Students-Parents-Louise-Webber/dp/1980411689/ref=sr_1_1?s=books&ie=UTF8&qid=153338238 3&sr=1-1&keywords=apprenticeships

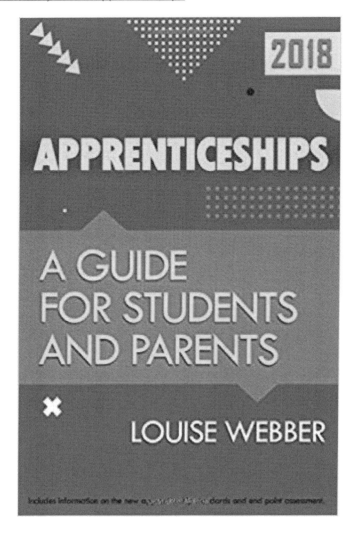

20 ACKNOWLEGEMENTS

I would like to thank my loving family and friends for all their support and the fantastic colleagues and friends I have at The Apprenticeship Centre, who strive to ensure all learners succeed and develop within their Apprenticeship courses.

I dedicate this book to my lovely daughters who brighten my life each and every day.

Thank you for taking the time to read this book. I hope you have gained some valuable information to support you in preparation for your end point assessment. If you have learned anything from this book and it has helped you, I would really appreciate it if you could leave a review of the book on Amazon as this helps others to understand what it is about and how it could help them too.

Thanks

Louise.

21 DISCLAIMER

Every effort has been made to ensure the currency, validity and accuracy of information contained within this book, however the publisher, author and editor cannot be held responsible for any errors or omissions, however caused.

No responsibility for loss or damage occasioned by any person acting or otherwise, as a result of information contained within this book, can be accepted by the author, editor or publisher.

This book was published independently of The Apprenticeship Centre and Apprenticeship EPA Centre and associated businesses.

Centre processes may vary. EPAO centres use their own systems of grading work and whilst this guide is there to support you, it cannot comprehensively cover every eventuality of questioning and/or formatting of end point assessment as each end point assessment centre have been tasked by the ESFA to create their own mark scheme and resources.

22 FIRST PUBLISHING DATE

This book was first published in October 2018.

23 REGISTER OF END POINT ASSESSMENT ORGANISATIONS

The register of end point assessment organisations details all the companies that offer EPA. Click the link below then follow the prompts for more information.

https://www.gov.uk/guidance/register-of-end-point-assessment-organisations

To check for the most up to date information on available Apprenticeship standards go to https://www.gov.uk/government/publications/apprenticeship-standards-list-of-occupations-available--2

48907274R00066

Printed in Poland
by Amazon Fulfillment
Poland Sp. z o.o., Wrocław